101

things to do during a
Dull Sermon

TIM SIMS WITH MARTIN WROE AND ADRIAN REITH

with a Little Help from:

RICKY CHRISTIAN • WILL EISENHOWER • TOM FINLEY
DAVID LYNN • DOUG PETERSON • ROBERT PRICE AND MIKE YACONELLI

MONARCH
BOOKS
Mill Hill, London & Grand Rapids, Michigan

First published by Monarch Books in the UK in 1988.
Reprinted in 1988, 1989. Reissued in 2002.
Concorde House, Grenville Place, Mill Hill, London NW7 3SA.

Reprinted 2003.

Published in the USA by Monarch Books in 2002.

Text illustrations by Dan Pegoda

Distributed by:
UK: STL, PO Box 300, Kingstown Broadway, Carlisle, Cumbria CA3 0QS;
USA: Kregel Publications, PO Box 2607, Grand Rapids, Michigan 49501.

ISBN 1 85424 549 X

British Library Cataloguing Data
A catalogue record for this book is available from the British Library.

Designed and produced for the publisher by
Gazelle Creative Productions,
Concorde House, Grenville Place, Mill Hill, London NW7 3SA.

Contents

Foreword

Church is pretty good... most of the time. And, no matter what anyone says, sermons are OK too... most of the time. Periodically, however, something goes wrong. Your minister has an off-day, and the sermon ends up... well... a little dull.

It's no one's fault, really. Maybe your minister didn't have enough time to study this week. Maybe your minister had an argument with his wife. Or her husband. It doesn't matter, because, whatever the reason, the result is the same: a dull sermon.

The question is: "What can you do about it?" Well. You could ask the minister to resign. But that takes a lot of time and energy and, unless dull sermons happen all the time, the problem may not be your minister. After all, your minister is a human being, subject to the same lapses that happen to all of us.

So, now we are back to the question, "What can you do about it?" That's a good question and this book has a lot of good answers. 101 of them actually. Each and every one of them will keep you, your family and the people sitting next to you in church occupied for many a dull sermon to come.

In fact, we have the feeling that after you use this book for a while, you will be looking forward to the next dull sermon. There are seven different categories of things to do (Higher Learning, Games, Diversions, Musings and Meditations, Fine Arts, Church-er-cise, and Fact and Figures). Most of the ideas in this book can be shared with those sitting around you, so they can "enjoy" the sermon, too.

Not only can the suggestions in this book keep you and yours occupied during the dull times, but you might even give a copy of this book to your minister. That might be just the motivation he needs to stop those dull sermons ever happening again.

PS. In case anything in this book offends you (and we hope it doesn't) we recommend that you turn immediately to item 101.

Higher Learning

Stimulating your mind when
the sermon doesn't

7

Jots and tittles

Locate all the typing ~~misteaks~~ mistakes in the church bulletin. Allow yourself extra points for bad grammar. (Q: Is syntax a sin?)

2

Word power

It pays to increase your word power, so they say. Whenever you hear a word you are unfamiliar with during the sermon, write it down and guess at a definition (that's how some theologians arrive at *their* definitions). Check your guesses with a dictionary, Bible dictionary or theological encyclopedia. Don't be too noisy turning the pages.

3 & 4

A modest proposal

Write a letter to the church council or elders proposing a lottery scheme to help finance the new building project. Be certain you have done adequate research by playing the game a few times yourself before making your proposal. (Deduct your losses from income tax by describing your activity as charitable religious research.)

Bird brain

See how many bird names you can list. Match the birds you have listed with church members who look or sound like them. Attract their attention with the relevant mating-call.

Six days you shall labour

Since many people in your congregation only work five days a week, devise a suitable list of jobs for the sixth day and submit it to them after church. Job ideas might include ironing the vicar's poodle or drycleaning the organist's toupée.

6

Hymn memorization

Instead of a short sleep you may like to
learn those troublesome third verses of
hymns — you know, the words that don't
scan, that you mumble as you try and
keep up with the new and unfamiliar
tune. Alternatively, translate the whole
hymn into Swahili.

Methuselah

See how many words you can make out of the word Methuselah.

Score:

1–9 words	Some boring spots in sermon
10–20 words	Lots of boring spots in sermon
21–40 words	Utterly boring sermon
41 or more words	Even the minister is bored and has decided to help you

8

Go tell it on the mountain

Compose a letter to your preacher extolling the spiritual rewards to be had on a solitary camping expedition. Then offer to loan him all your camping gear if he will take off for a few weeks.

Multiple choice church quiz

Answer the tough question below. In front of you in your pew there is probably a shelf for hymn books and all the bits of paper they give you when you walk in. In many non-Anglican churches you will find mysterious 2 cm (3/4") holes drilled or mounted in front of you. What are these holes for? Tick correct answer below:

A. Digital Support Socket. To assist the sleepy worshipper to stand at the right moment. (Insert two digits and pull.)

B. Church Notice-sheet Restrainer. An elaborate

device in which the church notice-sheet should be mounted to stop it falling on the floor as you doze.

C. Evidence of ferocious Death Watch Beetle.

D. Breathing holes for congregation when in the slumped-forward-in-prayer position.

E. All of the above.

(Answer: E.)

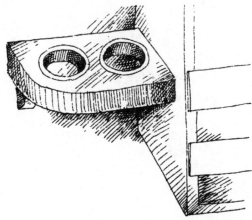

10

Song of Solomon

Using the Old Testament book The Song of Solomon as your guide, compose a love letter to a prominent church member. Leave it (unsigned, of course) inside a hymn book. Your gushy literary effort will keep you awake this week... and pep somebody up next Sunday.

11 & 12

Ananias and Sapphira List

List the names of the "Ten Most Likely to Be Struck Dead During the Offering".

In my arm his handiwork I see

With the freckles on your arm, make up some new constellations and name them. Advanced suggestion: See if you can find someone with freckles on *their* arm close enough for you to make up new constellations and name them. (Note: you can use your face, if you have a mirror, or you can focus your mirror on someone *else's* face.)

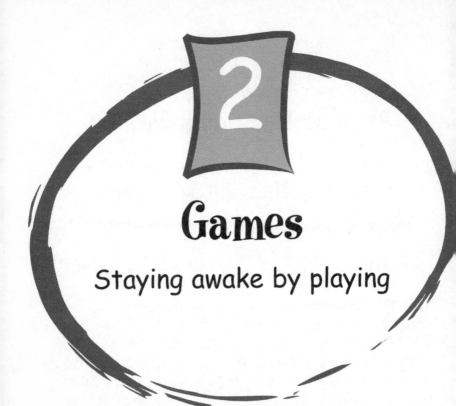

2

Games

Staying awake by playing

Alpha to omega

Listen for your preacher to use a word beginning with "A" then "B" and so on through the alphabet. You may get stuck on "X" unless it's December.

Armageddon-outta-here

When you hear any of the words or phrases in the grid below during the minister's sermon, mark the square with an "X". When you have five in a row in any direction, stand up and shout, "It's the rapture!"

LAST DAYS	WARS	CREDIT CARDS	EZEKIEL	144,000
EEC	TRUMPET	ANTICHRIST	TRIBULATION	REVELATION
DANIEL	THE BOMB	HAL LINDSEY	BABYLON	SIGNS
BOB MARLEY	DRUGS	AIDS	666	BEAST
CAUGHT UP	BANKS CRASH	ISRAEL	THIEF	1,000 YEARS

15 & 16

A-Millennial bingo

Wait for someone playing "Armageddon-outta-here" to stand up and shout, "It's the rapture!" Then stand up and shout, "No, it's not!"

Cast lots

All you need are knee pads, some dice, your offering money and… well, maybe this isn't such a good idea.

Biblevision

Create a rebus using the sermon text for the day. Example: "Lighten my eyes, lest I sleep the sleep of death" (Psalm 13:3).

 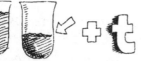 + t

 THE

OF

18

Who will be the next Pope?

See if you can find the identity of the next Pope
hidden in the letters below. It may be spelled
horizontally, vertically, diagonally, forward or
backward. If it is the name of the person sitting
behind you, get their autograph. If it is the
preacher, set up a new tourist industry.

```
Q W E R T Y U I O P A S D F G H J K L
F R E D G T H Y U J I K O L P W D E S
C F G V B I L L V A L E R I E T Y U O
E T H E L R E D B G M K I L O F G B N
W I L L I A M S W R O E R E I T H B M
C V B N M W E R T Y U I O P L K J H N
V C B N H M J Y T R D F C V D B G T T
S N I L L O C T T O T S E A W T U I O
C Z A X W E R T F G B V D C S A W S E
```

Hands up

If you are part of a lively congregation where there is a lot of hand raising, try cataloguing the various styles of raising hands as you observe them during the sermon.

People who use this "two-arm toss" position probably have been moved by one of the sermon points... either that or they are listening to football on a transistor radio and someone has just scored a goal.

This is a popular position, although it doesn't show quite the same level of uninhibited spontaneity as the two-arm toss. Also, if the arm is raised at an angle and the palm of his or her hand is facing down, you'd better check whether the worshipper is a traffic cop.

This means the heating's broken again.

"You have a ladder in your stockings. Can't you dress better for church?"

This means "illegal headcovering: there is a woman in church wearing the most ridiculous hat I've ever seen."

This quickly conveys the message, "Darling, it's your turn to shout at the kids."

"No dearest, I think it's your turn to discipline the brats."

"I'm desperate for the toilet."

20

Jumbled context

Open your Bible at random and point to a verse. Write it down. Repeat the process until you've received a personal message from Scripture. Example: "Pay their expenses so that they may shave their heads... (Acts 21:24) ...and your Father who sees in secret will reward you" (Matthew 6:18).

21

Pew warming

By experimentation, try to determine how many comfortable pew sitting positions you can discover. (You will kill a lot of time before you realize there are no comfortable pew sitting positions.)

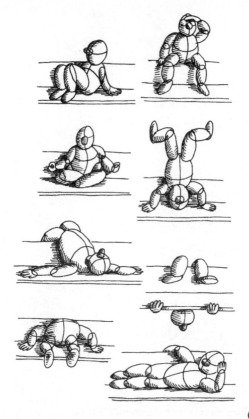

22

Marble roll

Sit in the back pew and roll a handful of marbles under the pews ahead of you. After the service, credit yourself with ten points for each marble that made it to the front.

23

Footsie with a twist

Play footsie with the person in front of you. If he or she turns round, shake your head and point to the person next to you. Give that person a disgusted look.

24

Baptism by force

Tuck a water pistol up your sleeve. See how many people you can forcibly baptize before they realize it is you. (For best results, sit in the front row of the balcony and shoot down.)

Flash cards

Make a set of score flash cards like the ones Olympic judges use to score sporting events. Judge this week's sermon on these categories:

1. Quality of monotone.
2. Use of obscure vocabulary.
3. Lack of interesting illustrations.
4. Number of irrelevant points.

26
Cartography

This is a traditional game that has entertained bored parishioners down through the centuries. Simply turn to the back of your Bible and pass the time by reading the maps there. Try adding some funny place names to "Paul's Missionary Travels" like Siberia and Tijuana, Mexico. You can bring the maps up to date by adding anti-aircraft gun emplacements in Iran and Russian SAM missiles in Syria.

27

How observant are you?

Look all around you for exactly ten seconds.
Now, close your eyes and then answer these
questions:
A. How many people are sitting in the pew with
   you?
B. What row are you sitting in?
C. What is the preacher wearing?
D. What colour are the walls?
E. What is the title of this book?
F. How can you read these questions with your
   eyes closed?

3

Diversions

A collection of slightly
disruptive activities

28 & 29

Pinch (first variation)

Modestly, discreetly and with the utmost decorum, pinch yourself to stay awake.

Pinch (second variation)

Modestly, discreetly and with the utmost decorum, pinch your neighbour. This should keep both of you awake.

Bible commentary

If you are sitting at the back of the church away from people, quietly "broadcast" the sermon (or the entire service) using the jargon of a sports commentator.

"THERE'S A SHARP BLOW TO THE CONGREGATION'S CONSCIENCE... ANOTHER HARD SHOT... THE PREACHER'S A WILD MAN OUT THERE... NOW HE TURNS AWAY... HE'S SHADOW BOXING NOW, THROWING PUNCHES AT AN OPPONENT WHO ISN'T REALLY THERE... HE'D HAVE THOSE LIBERALS UP AGAINST THE ROPE IF THEY'D STEP INSIDE THE RING... LOOK AT THAT FANCY FOOTWORK, SIDESTEPPING AN EMBARRASSING QUESTION...THERE'S THE BELL, SOUNDING THE END OF POINT TWO...!"

31

Clerical fashion spotting

An exercise in fashion-aesthetics. Work out whether your vicar is wearing bell-bottoms under his cassock. As he walks up to the pulpit or wobbles behind the lectern during his sermon and his dressage rises up, try and spot what — if anything — he is wearing under the clerical garb.

(A pair of 1972 flared Levi jeans will not be unusual. Bare ankles and calfs could indicate that your minister is more interesting than his sermons.)

32 & 33

Missionary pilot

Using church notice-sheets or newcomer's cards for raw materials, design, test and modify a collection of paper airplanes.

Rumble

Listen for rumbling stomachs. Count how many different kinds of rumble you can hear. Time them to see which goes on the longest.

Yawn

See if a yawn really is contagious.

Breath control

Time yourself holding your breath. You may wish to keep records from week to week to note your improvement.

36 & 37

Request

Pass a note to the organist asking whether he or she plays requests.

Choral distraction

Any number of techniques can be used to create laughter behind the preacher's back, but care must be taken lest you are discovered and reprimanded from the pulpit. This is a definite improvement on an old diversion: watching the choir members trying to stay awake.

38

Anonymous letter

Requires scissors and glue. Cut out individual letters from notice-sheets, hymn books etc. and arrange them into an anonymous note (remember the ransom notes in old films?). In the letter (to be sent to the preacher) suggest guest speakers or candidates to replace him in the pulpit.

39 & 40

Cue cards, first variation

Help the preacher by giving him a responsive audience. From the front pew hold up large cards that will help the listeners to respond in unison (as in the old silent films). Sample cards: "Amen", "I hear you", "That's right", "Ha ha ha", "Ooooh" etc.

Cue cards, second variation

Similar to the previous diversion, only these cards are designed to help the preacher keep in touch with the moods of the audience. Sample cards: "Get to the point", "Tell another joke", "You're fading fast", "We're praying for you" etc.

41 & 42

To Bernie or not to Bernie

Pass a note to someone called Bernie, but first make sure there is no one called Bernie in your congregation. (Note: if you are in a synagogue, try the name "Ricardò".)

Pew crawl

Start from the back of the church and try to crawl all the way to the front, under the pews, without being noticed.

43

Snuff out the sermon

About four minutes into the sermon, when everyone's asleep, insert a little snuff up your right nostril. Just as your sneeze is ready, take a deep breath and convert it into an atomic explosion from your face. This should induce at least one heart attack and the emergency services will terminate the sermon mid-ramble.

(NB Only attempt this in congregations of more than two otherwise there won't be anyone to get palpitations next week.)

44 & 45

Potty break

Raise your hand and ask for permission to go to the lavatory.

Turn the other cheek

Slap your neighbour. See if he or she turns the other cheek. If not, raise your hand and tell the pastor.

46 & 47

Contemplative snoozing

Learn to sleep while kneeling. If someone wakes you up, simply say, "Amen", and they will be embarrassed that they disturbed you.

Prayer request cards

Using the prayer request cards located in the rack of the pew in front of you, compose some rather juicy little pieces concerning absurd habits, alien abductions or some shocking confession. Don't sign a name... or, on second thought, sign someone else's name.

48

Misplaced Amen

Shout a loud "Amen!" at the
conclusion of a sentence that isn't
particularly inspiring. Wait and see
if anyone else chimes in with an
"Amen!" or if the sermon suddenly
becomes livelier in response to your
response.

49

Last of the red hot sermons

As a creative way to earn money during a dull sermon, walk among the congregation with a tray of hot dogs and shout, "Hot dogs! Get your hot dogs here!" To help create the right atmosphere, you could start a Mexican wave, and the organist could play the Olympics theme.

50 & 51

Wristwatch alarm

Once the minister begins his sermon, set the alarm of your watch to beep after twenty minutes ... and every five minutes thereafter until he has finished.

Applause

Though you are sleepy, loudly applaud the minister at the conclusion of his sermon. He'll think he made a vivid impact on your life. As an exercise of Christian charity, keep the *real* reason to yourself.

52

Liberal church altar call

If you are at a liberal church, come forward to be "born-again" towards the end of the sermon, that will really throw things into a tizzy. It may even start a revival.

Nasal hymns

Whip out a handkerchief and blow your nose. Vary the pressure exerted on your nostrils and trumpet a rendition of your favourite hymn.

54 & 55

Better to receive

Bring along an offering plate and start passing it round during the sermon. Then quietly change your seat so the offering plate comes back to you, full.

Losing contact

Blink and squint dramatically, then get down on your hands and knees. If the person next to you asks what the matter is, tell him you've just lost your contact lens. Crawl quickly towards the door.

56

Creative endings

If the sermon is droning on far too long, take things into your own hands for a quick finish:

A. Pretend to pass out; slump unconscious onto the aisle floor.
B. Begin sneezing uncontrollably (this may, however, result in an attempted exorcism).

Smelly socks

Refrain from washing your socks for eleven days. During the sermon, remove your shoes.
WARNING: Don't bother if your minister hasn't yet received the gift of smell.

58 & 59

Alarm

Unravel a thread from the back of a hymn book. Tie one end to the pew in front of you and the other end to your wrist. As the congregation leaves, someone will break or trip over the thread, thus alerting you in time to exit with the crowd.

Forever blowing bubbles

If the sermon goes on for more than fifteen minutes, start blowing bubbles.

Amazing gaze

Stare intently at the preacher.
Count how many times the
preacher looks into your eyes.
See if you can make him
sweat.

61

Hearing-aid humming

Sit in the hearing-aid section of the church building. During the sermon, whisper to several old folks that the preacher wants everyone to hum. Begin humming "Amazing Grace" and encourage all the hard-of-hearing saints of the Lord who are sitting near you (and can't hear the message anyway) to hum along.

62

Baptismal surprise

Hide in the font or baptistry wearing a "creature from the black lagoon" outfit. Stay out of sight, but softly begin calling the pastor by name. When the preacher finally stops his sermon and comes over to see who is calling, grab his tie and see if you can pull him in.

63

Hymn bricks

Using your own and your neighbours'
hymn books, build a model of your
church. Borrow more hymn books as
necessary. If your church is particularly
large, ask your neighbours to help you
get reserve stocks from the church
cupboard. With a little imagination you
can get the whole congregation to help
you improve the design.

64

Quick and easy

A. By unobtrusively drawing your arms up your sleeves, turn your shirt or blouse inside out.

B. Try to raise one eyebrow.

C. Crack your knuckles.

D. Since it's obvious that your minister does not come from the same planet as you, decide where he'd be more at home. Mars? Venus? A black hole?

E. If you have a retractable ball-point pen, take it apart and shoot the ink cartridge straight up into the air with the spring.

F. Make an empty chewing gum wrapper look as if

there's still gum in it. Fool the person next to you.
G. Pretend to be four years old.
H. Guess how many angels can dance on the end of a pin.
I. Guess how many angels can dance on the end of your nose.
J. See how many categories of nose you can find: fat noses, pointed noses, flat noses etc.
K. Try to indicate to the minister that his fly is open.
L. Come to church wearing your swim suit under your clothes. During the sermon remove your outer clothes so that only your swim suit is on, so you are ready to go to the beach as soon as the sermon is over.
M. Try to guess what the sidesmen are doing in the vestry.
N. Join the sidesmen in the vestry.

O. Think about your chin(s) for an entire minute.
P. Twiddle your thumbs.
Q. Twiddle your neighbour's thumbs.
R. Get everyone in your row to twiddle their thumbs.
S. Keep shaking your head "no" as if violently disagreeing with everything the minister is saying. See how long it takes to distract him.
T. Wiggle your ears so that the people behind you will notice.
U. Wiggle the ears of the person in front of you.
V. Duck as they lash out at you.
W. Drop a hymn book and count how many people turn round to see where the sound came from.
X. Practise smiling insincerely.
Y. Try to think of another "quick and easy" thing to do so we'll have a full alphabet's worth — from a to z.
Z. Write it in here: _____

4

Musings and Meditations
Creative use of the imagination

83

Blessed are they that thirst

The Bible has strong words to say about those who "oppress". Think about how you might organize the masses in protest against the "killer coffee" served after the service. Who of those sitting around you has the inspirational qualities to lead such an insurrection? How about interrupting the minister now by shouting, "Either the coffee goes or I do!" Then walk out, the thirsty victor.

66

Comforting comparison

List some things that would be even *more*
boring than listening to this dull sermon,
for example:

A. Writing this year's Christmas list.
B. Balancing your bank account.
C. Cleaning your comb.
D. Humming an Andy Williams song.

67

Ecclesiastical rhyming slang

Consider the rhyming lines in today's hymns. Decide which rhyming word came first (ie which the writer wanted to use) and which came second. (Clue: This will be the drivel line which sacrifices integrity, humanity, truth and art to achieve its aim.) Eg:

> Lord, we want to praise your name,
> Yesterday, today, for ever... er... the same.
> Lord, we just really praise your name,
> Lord in the sun, Lord through the rain.

Anon. (And we know why.)

68

Creative responsive readings

Come up with some new responsive readings for your congregation. An example might be:

PASTOR: Hello Dolly, well Hello Dolly.
CONGREGATION: It's so nice to have you back where you belong.
PASTOR: You're looking swell, Dolly.
CONGREGATION: We can tell, Dolly.
PASTOR: You're still growing, you're still showing, you're still going strong.
CONGREGATION: And also with you.

69 & 70

Zacchaeus

Devise ways of climbing into the balcony without using the stairs.

Getting the picture

Keep your mind in touch with the sermon by outlining it with illustrations. Use simple cartoons, even stick figures, to capture the ideas.

JOSEPH and MARY'S FLIGHT TO EGYPT

Ink blot test

Make ink blots on the notice-sheet and ask a friend to guess what they represent. Now analyse your friend's responses and suggest that he see a psychiatrist.

72 & 73

Blairize

Carefully listen to each word the preacher says, but imagine how it would sound if Tony Blair was speaking. Try not to burst out laughing.

The Bible study

Read Acts 20:7–12. Ring any bells?

a) When did you last hear this passage expounded in your church? (Be careful in answering, you may just have been asleep.)

b) Is there a need in your church for a "Eutychus Group" to act as a watch-dog on timing?

Psalming

When the preacher makes a dramatic or melodramatic statement, complete it with a rhyming phrase. The more ridiculous, the better.

Example: Pastor: "We count people because people count", then you add, "and our rivals are impressed with our amount." *Or:* Pastor: "God helps those who help themselves", then you add, "and our fairy cakes are baked by elves." *Or:* Pastor: "To join this church you've gotta believe", then you add, "and empty your pockets when the offering's received."

5

Fine Arts

Handling boredom
with finesse

75 & 76

Keep an eye peeled

Use felt pens to colour false eyeballs on your eyelids. People will think you're wide awake through the whole sermon.

Loud, have mercy

Build a remote control for the church sound system and when you start to get tired of the sermon, very gradually turn the volume up until the sermon stops... or everyone has evacuated the building.

What child is this?

On the Sunday before, "accidentally" take home a hymn book. Hollow out the pages as they do in spy films and fit in a miniature tape recorder. Make a tape of a baby crying. Then go to church with the modified hymn book and wait for the right moment. Once the sermon has begun, discreetly begin the tape. Make sure the crying doesn't begin straightaway but perhaps five minutes into the cassette so it seems to have started on its own. Also, make sure the volume is turned up loud enough so it can be heard through the book cover. With the hymn book in its rack and you sitting back in the pew, no one will be able to guess whose child is causing all the rumpus.

Nail sculpture

Clip your nails. Use the clippings to make little "fish" symbols on the back of the pew in front of you.

Glowing sermon

Have you ever noticed that if you leave your eyes wide open as long as possible without blinking, you will see the walls change colour and the preacher outlined in fluorescent white? Shapes will shift and change, hues will flash and sparkle.

It's fun, try it... but don't go overboard.

We don't want your eyes to turn into dried-out raisins.

80

Fake head trick

During the week, take some time to sculpt and paint an exact likeness of your head. While in church wear the fake head on top of your shoulders. Your real head will be down inside your jacket and you will be free to sleep or, if you bring a flashlight you can read the Sunday paper. If you are a particularly clever artist, you may want to try the Fake Head and Body Trick which would leave you free for a coffee in town.

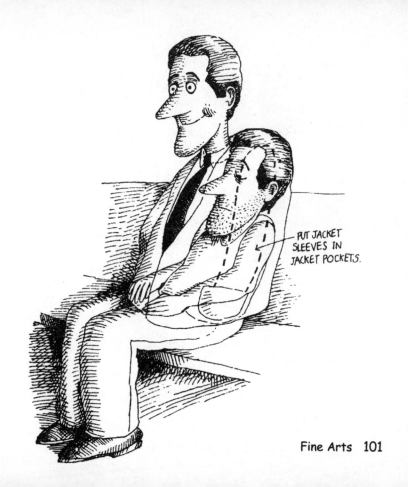

Fine Arts 101

81 & 82

The which underwear test

Ascertain by careful inspection whether your minister is wearing boxers, briefs, long johns (rare: award yourself extra points) or another variety of underwear. What does this tell you about their theological foundations?

Remember

Try to remember what last week's sermon was about. Try to remember what this week's sermon is about. Try to remember the last time the preacher didn't mention money.

6

Church-er-cise

Aerobics for the
church pew

Finger twirl

Move your left index finger in a circle clockwise three times. After some practice, try moving the same finger in the opposite direction.

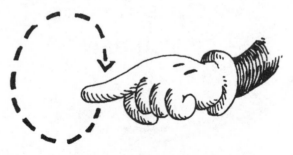

Rear-ender

Indicate with your two index fingers two points on the pew 12 centimetres (five inches) away from your body to the left and right of you. Then race your bottom back and forth between the two points. Hold a short ceremony to celebrate the winner.

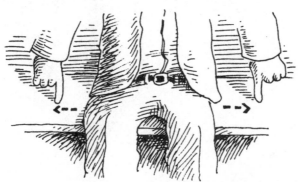

Lip lick

Lick your lips.

Foot feat

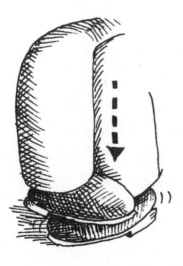

Step on your left foot with your right foot while trying to raise your left foot off the ground.

87

Weight lifting

Even dull pastors love firm
believers, so make good use of the
house. Take two hymn books in
each hand and practise arm thrusts
and curls. Great for the biceps.
Hook your toes beneath the pew in
front of you and perform leg lifts.

Church-er-cise 109

88

Teeth-totalling

Count your teeth with your tongue. Count your tongue with your teeth.

7

Facts and Figures

Mathematical diversions
to keep you awake

89

The hairs on your head are numbered

Yes, but do you know the number? Try counting them during the sermon. If there are too many to count on one Sunday, divide it up and count only those hairs on one side of your parting. A variation on this activity, suitable for upper middle class congregations, is to count the number of toupées.

90

1,000 years

If, in the Lord's sight, a day is as a thousand years and a thousand years is as a day, how many years would this sermon be consuming if it were a thousand-year day? Share your answer with the pastor.

Counting

A. Count new hair-cuts.
B. Count people who need new hair-cuts.
C. Count babies you like.
D. Count babies you don't like.
E. Count your ribs.
F. Count your neighbour's ribs.
G. Count your black eyes after counting your neighbour's ribs.
H. Count bald heads.
I. Count your teeth fillings.
J. Count the number of times you change position during today's sermon.
K. Count how many dead animals the women in the church are wearing.

L. Count how many of their husbands look like dead animals.
M. Count everyone in the balcony. Calculate how many people in the balcony it would take to make the floor collapse.
N. Count how many people in the choir should never be allowed to sing... anywhere.
O. Count how many things you wish you were doing right now.

P. Calculate how much money you would pay the minister to stop preaching.

Q. Count the pieces of gum underneath your pew.

R. Count the little kids underneath your pew.

S. Count the entire congregation.

T. Count the number of people in the congregation who are not listening to the sermon either. Maybe it would be faster to count the number of people still listening to the sermon.

U. Calculate how many pages of your latest novel you would have got through if you could have been reading right now.

V. Count how many times you have thought about leaving the church.

W. Count the organ pipes.

X. Count the songs in the hymn book that you don't understand.

Y. Count the number of times your minister has said "in closing" in today's sermon.

Z. Count people counting.

92 & 93

Ecclesiastical challenge

Find a line in a song from the hymn book that more devastatingly defeats its own object than the line: "So forget about yourself, concentrate on him and worship him" — repeated three times.

Psychosermatics

Consider the mechanics of this dull sermon: just *what* about it is *so* boring? a) the tone of voice? b) the number of words? c) the content? d) the speed of delivery (or lack of it)? e) all four? (You may want to hand in your assessment to the preacher at the end. This is not compulsory.)

94

Weeping and wailing

When one baby in an otherwise silent congregation begins crying loudly, other babies will often join in. By getting the baby nearest to you to start crying (take away his dummy, make ugly faces etc), see how many other babies you can get to cry all at the same time. Count the babies crying and compare with the number that a friend can make cry during the next lull. Highest number wins. Score bonus points if you can make the preacher cry.

Choir scales

Guess the weight of each member of the choir. This may be difficult since most choir robes look like circus tents. Place bets and compare results with the person next to you. Then, query each choir member after the service to determine who had the closest guess.

96

Calling Dr Luke

Count the number of people who cough or clear their throats. An interesting study is to calculate a coughs-per-minute ratio and compare it to the coughs-per-minute ratio during the prayer time or the announcements.

97 & 98

Creative visitor embarrassment

List ways to embarrass visitors. It will be difficult to think of things that churches haven't done already, but try. (Here are some suggestions to get the creative juices going: have the visitor list all the books of the Bible by memory; ask the visitor why he/she hasn't been coming to church.)

Ego tally

Keep weekly figures on the number of times the preacher says "I", uses a personal illustration, or gives a personal opinion.

99
Clothes call

Look around and see how many mistakes in clothing you can find. For example, are there any inside-out socks, shirts or gloves? How about collars that need turning down, buttons misbuttoned, stockings with ladders or shoes untied? Oh, by the way, be careful not to look *too* hard at a couple of these.

100 & 101

Preacher's salary

Estimate the preacher's salary and calculate the amount he/she is making for each minute of the sermon.

101 things sequel

Think of 101 people who take life entirely too seriously. Buy each of them this book.